CONCANNON

THE FIRST ONE HUNDRED AND TWENTY-FIVE YEARS

JIM CONCANNON WITH TIM PATTERSON · PHOTOGRAPHS BY ANDY KATZ

Published in 2006 by Andy Katz Photography
4982 West Soda Rock Lane
Healdsburg, CA 95448
(707) 433-9396
www.andykatzphotography.com

Library of Congress
Cataloging-in-Publication Data:
Concannon: The First One Hundred and Twenty-Five Years
ISBN 0-9649805-8-4

Printing: Mondadori, Verona, Italy

First Edition

10 9 8 7 6 5 4 3 2 1

Book Design: Soda Rock Studios, Healdsburg, CA
www.sodarockstudios.com

Without the help of the following people I would not have been able to produce this book

Jim and Helen Concannon --
for their kindness and good humor throughout

David Kent --
who had the confidence and trust to let me produce this wonderful book

Ellen Riendeau --
for her brilliant design and feedback

Tim Patterson --
for his excellent prose

And I especially want to thank Lynn Kirimli for her tremendous support, patience, and determination to make the book the best it could be

I toast all with a wonderful glass of Concannon wine

Andy Katz

To my grandparents, James and Ellen Concannon --
For their vision and desire to seek America as their new homeland, bringing with them their rich Irish heritage

To my parents, Joseph and Nina Concannon --
For teaching by example their strong faith, dedication, and sense of service to our church, country, community and one another

To my late brother Joe and sister Marie, my sister-in-law Peggy and sister Nina and their families

To my wife Helen --
For encouragement and support the last forty-six years and the joy in raising our family

Most importantly to our children John, Mary, Anna Marie and Paul, and our grandchildren Shannon, Eric and Kyle Patrick

The pride and joy you have given me is truly the gift called family

Jim Concannon
April 20, 2006

CONTENTS

ACKNOWLEDGEMENTS

Most of this book is based on one man's memory, and for good reason. The intent was to capture and preserve a piece of California winemaking history in the form of a personal tale wrapped in exuberant photography, not to produce a scholarly volume. In the interests of accuracy, completeness and context, however, a number of individuals and institutions were consulted on one topic or another, and their ready assistance shows throughout these pages. Anything we got wrong, we got wrong on our own.

Thanks to Robert Zerkowicz, librarian at The Wine Institute in San Francisco; to Susan Nelson-Kluk at Foundation Plant Services at the University of California at Davis, John Duarte of Duarte Nursery, Chris Lindelof of Grey Creek Viticultural Services, Andy Bledsoe of Vintage Wine Trust and Jo Diaz of PS I Love You for help in tracing the "Concannon clones"; to Gary Sehnert of Wines of Mexico, José Milmo of Casa Madero in Coahuila, Mexico, and Mexican wine historian Rondi Frankel for insights into the fate of the vines James Concannon shipped across the border; to former Concannon winemakers Sergio Traverso and Tom Lane for their perspective on the Livermore Valley and on their years in the cellar; to current winemaker Adam Richardson for illuminating Concannon's wine philosophy today; to the entire Wente family for generations of friendship and a common devotion to the potential of the Livermore Valley, and to Phil and Eric in particular for background on events in this book; and to Livermore historian Gary Drummond for all his work over the years to document not only the early years at Concannon but the founding of the whole Livermore Valley wine culture.

Thanks to members of the Concannon family who contributed through interviews—Helen Concannon, Peggy Concannon and Nina Concannon Radisch—and to the others who contributed moral support for the project. Helen, as usual, performed minor miracles behind the scenes that kept things moving.

Thanks to Nancy Freeman for her eagle-eyed copyediting. And finally, thanks to Lynn Kirimli, without whose enthusiasm, vision and project management this book never would have happened.

Jim Concannon
Tim Patterson
April, 2006

FOREWORD

The California wine community has achieved a deserved reputation for producing world-class wine. Concurrently, it has earned equal recognition for its years of social responsibility and great commitment to sustainability programs and stewardship of the land. It is clear this acclaim did not come about overnight, but emerges from the rich heritage of individual, family and entrepreneurial dedication to ethical values and high technical standards.

The wonderful explosion of new wineries, new consumers and new media coverage should not obscure, nor diminish, the significance and continuing contribution of those families who built the early and strong foundation for global competitiveness. In this context, we welcome and applaud the publication of "Concannon: The First One Hundred and Twenty-Five Years." The engagingly informative and personal tales by Jim Concannon with Tim Patterson, and the magnificent photos by Andy Katz, will rejuvenate our knowledge of the past, which in

turn illuminates the present period. The old axiom truly applies: "You really can't know where you are going if you don't know where you've been."

Jim Concannon's reflections encouraged my own personal memories. In February 1976, shortly after becoming President and CEO of Wine Institute, I gave an inaugural address to the California Association of Winegrape Growers. My wife Josephine and I had the good fortune to sit next to Joe Concannon for lunch. He commended us for appearing together and said, "You know families are both the backbone and the inspiration for our industry. And our wives are more important than the outside world appreciates." He extended an invitation to both of us to come visit Concannon Vineyard, which coincided with an equally gracious invitation by Karl and Jean Wente to visit their winery and home.

Our first visit to Livermore wine country, our walk through the rocky vineyards, and our tasting of their signature varietals, prompted an untutored question: "How could such fine grapes and wine come from such stony and austere land?" The response was the first time I heard the expression: "Struggle in the vineyards puts character in the bottle." Very soon after, I learned of another struggle that had forged personal strength.

Joe Concannon called to tell me that he had only a short time to live and wanted to prepare a smooth transition for his brother Jim to become a director of Wine Institute. To this day I am still taken by his quiet and calm demeanor and observation: "Generations may come and go but families must stay strong and committed." His was a genuine profile of love and courage.

My subsequent decades with Jim, and the entire Concannon family, led to insights and revelations that are well amplified in Jim's memoirs: the historic value of providing sacramental wines during Prohibition; the family's many years of international and commercial contacts; the Concannons' generosity in sharing vine cuttings of great varietal grapes with other vineyard regions; and the maintenance of the "Concannon Essence" through ownership changes.

The Irish-Italian heritage of the Concannons help explain the ecumenical history and added dynamism of Livermore's winegrowers and vintners. Their heritage is a pearl of great price that merits new appreciation. Under the leadership and companion culture of The Wine Group, Concannon's renaissance and revitalization are assured.

John A. De Luca, Ph.D.
Executive Vice Chairman
Wine Institute

JAMES CONCANNON (1847-1911)

THE LUCK OF THE IRISH

I never knew my grandfather, James Concannon, the founder of Concannon Vineyard. He died in 1911, twenty years before I was born. Stories about him got passed down through the family, and I'm sure some of them got tinkered with and stretched, maybe just made up over time. Other things I've learned from journalists and historians and people who've researched the subject in more depth than I have. We still have some old paperwork and photographs, fascinating stuff, though a lot of that has been lost, too.

But I know what he accomplished. I can look through the old pictures of his generation and my father's generation. I can walk through the house Grandfather built in 1883, where I grew up and where Helen and I raised our own children. Or I can just stroll through the vineyard picking up rocks, and I know what he left behind—not just a successful winery, but five generations of family.

I think what he did was amazing—to come to a strange country, knowing nothing about grapes or wine, raise a family of ten, and establish a winery that's been a pillar of the Livermore Valley for almost a hundred and twenty-five years. Every time I think about it, all I can say is … wow!

The Concannon clan goes back about a thousand years in Ireland; it may be one of the oldest family names in that country. In the 1600s, when the English occupied the Irish territory, the choice was to give up the Catholic faith or give up your land. My family said we'll give up our land. Eventually they settled forty miles off the coast of Galway Bay in the Aran Islands—far enough away it was hard for the British to get there.

When I went back to Ireland for the Concannon Millennium celebration in 1989, I was amazed to discover that the Aran Islands are even rockier than Livermore. Until recently, you could only get around in a Land Rover. I've been to the home my grandfather was born in, where my cousin now lives, and the walls are made from big, heavy rocks cleared from the land. There's just something about this family and rocks.

My grandfather was born on St. Patrick's Day, 1847, the youngest of five children. Maybe being born on that special day was the start of "the luck of the Irish" that seems to run in our family. In 1865, when he was eighteen, he heard that the Civil War was over in the United States and that it was safe to come over here. The reason for leaving was simple—opportunity— and Grandfather was clearly somebody who liked a challenge. His Uncle Peter—Peadar in Gaelic—who was a bachelor in Maine paid the way for my grandfather and one of his cousins.

His older sister, Bridget, had a special affection for him. When he said goodbye to depart for America, she gave him two gifts, a golden circlet from her finger and a golden guinea for his purse, so that he would never be in need. He kept the coin until his death and then gave it to his son Joseph, my father, who gave it to me before he died. The Concannons never got rich, but that guinea meant too much to ever spend. I still have it today.

Grandfather landed in New York on the steamship Webster in June, 1865. He went to Boston and got work like many immigrants at the Singer Sewing Machine Company, which wasn't much to his liking. So he moved to Augusta, Maine, where his uncle Peter lived, and got a job as a bellman at the Mansion House hotel.

JAMES AND ELLEN CONCANNON WITH THEIR TEN CHILDREN
1905

THE CONCANNON HOME
1900

The Concannon Coat of Arms

The Concannon family crest dates back several centuries, and was used for a while on some Concannon Vineyard wine labels. The motto—Con-Gan-On—was introduced during the Crusades and translates as "wisdom without blemish" or "wisdom without guile." The green oak on a mound of green is a heraldry symbol for hope, joy and loyalty; the oak also symbolizes plenty—the ability of its acorns to feed the animals. The falcon looks out over the countryside, ready to defend against the encroachment of the enemy. The crosses were added in recognition of service in two expeditions during the Crusades; the blue signifies loyalty and truth, and the fact that they are not red means no loss of life. The elephant symbolizes strength and courage—"Great strength, great wit and great ambition."

Augusta was the capital city, and the hotel was where a lot of the legislators and other important people stayed. My grandfather had the natural Irish way with people, and I think he learned a lot in those years. He continued his education and eventually became the manager.

He married an Irish girl, Ellen Rowe, in 1874. After their first child was born, they decided to move West, because it was wide open. The East was a tough place for the Irish and other immigrants in those days. But before they moved, he dug into his savings for a trip back to Ireland, to see the land and the family once more. While he was there, he discovered that some farmers on those rocky islands had managed to grow potatoes, a surplus in fact, and he found a way to market them on the mainland. Jumping on that opportunity paid for his trip, and he was able to replace the family's savings. Pretty enterprising fellow.

Somehow the story got spread that my grandparents came West in a covered wagon, but I think that's probably just spin. The train seems more likely to me. They settled in San Francisco, and he got a job with a local bookseller, Anton Roman, who published popular writers like Bret Harte. Then he got a franchise with SH Shepler in the rubber stamp business, first selling to a local territory and finally covering everything from the Canadian border into Mexico. Rubber stamps for offices were a huge craze for awhile, and that's where he made his money. And Mexico is also where he perfected his Spanish, which turned out to be important later on.

He and Grandmother were living in the Mission District in San Francisco, which was a good part Irish in those days. They no doubt went to Mass at Mission Dolores, where they became friends with Archbishop Alemany. The fact that Grandfather could converse with him in Español was probably a plus. Grandmother was already talking about getting out of the city and into the country air, and she also wanted him home more often and not always out on the road.

So it may have been Grandmother who talked to Alemany first. In any case, the archbishop eventually said to Grandfather, "I know you have this family and want to improve yourself, so why don't you get some land and produce sacramental wine for the Catholic Church?"

Always up for a challenge, he settled on Livermore, bought 47 acres of an old ranch in 1883, built a house, and started planting vines. That's where the story really begins.

HOE PLOW USED IN THE 1800'S

THE SHALALE USED BY JAMES CONCANNON TO WALK THE ROCKY VINEYARD

The First (Successful) Irish Vintner in America

When you think about the builders of America's wine culture and their origins, you're likely to conjure up Italian or German names—Mondavi, Sebastiani, Gallo, Martini, Beringer, Krug, Wente, Korbel. The Irish don't top the list. It's not that the Irish can't make wine; there is in Ireland an Order of Winegeese, with a large membership of winemakers who have left the country to make wine elsewhere. Jim Concannon was inducted as a Chevalier of the Order in the 1990s. But among the pioneering names in American wine, James Concannon has often been called the first Irish winemaker on these shores, and there's a big kernel of truth in that claim.

For the record, remember that immigrants started growing grapes and making wine on the eastern coast of the North American continent as soon as they landed in the 1600s, using both the abundant native varieties and imported European vines. For two hundred years, these pioneering efforts mostly failed, stymied by climate, disease and pests until well into the 19th century. No doubt more than one enterprising Irishman struggled in the mix.

In the decades just before the Civil War, when California was just becoming a state, the center of the wine industry was in the southland, in places like Riverside, Cucamonga, Anaheim, the San Fernando Valley and inside the city limits of Los Angeles itself. Among the major players in that speculative boom were a number with recognizably Irish surnames, like Matthew Keller and Andrew Boyle, from whom the Boyle Heights neighborhood of Los Angeles gets its designation. But between devastating diseases and a financial bubble, none of these ventures lasted more than a few years.

What sets James Concannon apart is that the vineyard he planted in 1883 and the wines he began producing soon thereafter have flourished for a century and a quarter, making it one of California's longest-lived wineries. James Concannon may not have been the first Irishman to make wine in America, but he was certainly the first to make a lasting success out of it. And that's no blarney.

PUTTING DOWN ROOTS

When Archbishop Alemany suggested the idea of planting a vineyard and making altar wine, Grandfather was probably shocked. It wasn't a business he knew well. And, for that matter, like a lot of people at the time, he'd taken the cold-water pledge to abstain from drinking—at least that's the story that's been passed down. But he was the kind of person who'd try almost anything within reason, and he had a good eye for a business opportunity.

The Church had kept records about the potential of California winegrowing regions from the time of the explorations by Juan Bautista de Anza and the arrival of the Mission padres in the 1770s. So Archbishop Alemany was able to suggest that the soils in the southern part of the Livermore Valley had the same rocky, gravelly character as parts of Bordeaux and the Rhône region in France. There was already some land planted in vineyards in the area by the time Grandfather arrived in 1883—the Wentes and the Concannons weren't the first. He bought a few acres to begin the operation, started clearing the land, and put his brother-in-law to work building the house. Not long after, he brought his brother Thomas over from Ireland to take charge of the rubber stamp business, and later his brother Martin to help with the vineyards.

I'm not sure what drew him to the particular parcel he bought, but it turned out to be one of the best places to grow grapes in the entire Valley. The original plantings were mainly white grapes, which the Church preferred for altar wine back then—among other things, white wines wouldn't stain the altar linens. Some cuttings came from local growers, some we know were ordered from France through Louis Mel, another vineyard pioneer right across the road, where Murrieta's Well is now. Mel's wife had connections with the owners of Château d'Yquem, the famous Sauternes producer in Bordeaux, and that was the source of some of the early Semillon and Sauvignon Blanc vines—not just for Grandfather, but for a number of vineyards in Livermore. Going to the trouble of getting those vines set the tone for the whole project by aiming for quality: if you're going to make wine, why not start with the best vines on earth?

In the early days, we used to bottle a wine called Chateau Y'Quem—a lot of other people at the time used French chateau names, too. Later when we dropped that name, we had Chateau Concannon, the same sweet white wine, from those same French vines, which was very popular for years and years.

I think those times set the tone for Livermore ever since—a spirit of cooperation, wineries sharing equipment and knowledge and grapevines, people looking out for each other. And of course socializing. It was a small number of families, but close. My Dad always used to tell about how the ten Concannon children and the eight Wente children would gather every morning on the road by our house and head into town together—they must have been half of the school!

Grandfather consulted the experts of the time to find out more about grapes and wine. He worked with Dr. Eugene Hilgard and Dr. Frederic Bioletti, the founders of the University of California viticulture and enology program, which had just started at UC Berkeley. He always sought out people who knew more about something than he did—he didn't just guess at things. He seemed to be able to acquire knowledge, in many different fields, very quickly.

The first vintage we know of was 1886, probably made in the basement—small amounts at first. As the years went on, he bought more vineyard land, ten acres here, twenty acres there, forty acres from the Wentes at one point. The first real winery facility was built in 1895 and was soon turning out 100,000 gallons of wine. Some of the wine was sold in bulk to the big San Francisco operations; some was for altar wine; and from the start, some of it was bottled under the Concannon label and sold to the public.

Not more than about ten years into the business, phylloxera, an insect that devours vine roots, spread from other parts of California and hit the vineyards in Livermore. That meant Grandfather had to replant, and so he personally went on two trips to France—this was around the Horn, before the Panama Canal—learning more about vineyards and winemaking and selecting vines. This time we know there were some reds in the mix, including Durif—Petite Sirah—from one supplier. The replanting took several years, and was completed just about the time he died in 1911.

In the middle of all this, the great San Francisco earthquake struck in 1906, and a lot of wine was spilled in cellars all over the Bay Area and the wine country. Grandfather sent my father Joseph out of the house to see what was going on with the winery. The ground was moving up and down. Trees were waving back and forth. It was a scary scene. Dad went into the winery and discovered we had lost not one drop of wine. When he came back and reported the good news, Grandfather responded that the Lord must have been looking out for us. He really believed that faith would get you through hard times.

With a large family, a winery in Livermore, and business interests in Mexico, Grandfather still kept up with what was happening in Ireland. A lot of Irish travelers came through the living room of our old house. The writer Seumas McManus came to visit at least twice; the bedrooms were full, so he slept in a couple of blankets rolled up by the fireplace. There were a lot of conversations in that living room about the situation over there. Grandfather was no revolutionary, and he didn't have a lot of money, but he had a lot of contacts. They wanted their country free; it was that simple.

I know that Grandfather's funeral was a major event in Livermore. Ernest Wente was one of the pallbearers. And I've been to this little museum in the Aran Islands, in Ireland, that has a section honoring my grandfather and displaying some bottles of Concannon wine. I may never have met him, but I know the kind of man he was.

ORIGINAL CONCANNON WINERY
1895

Boom Times in Livermore

In the 1880s and into the 1890s, the Livermore Valley was the hottest ticket in the California wine industry. Wine grapes had been grown there since the 1840s, but the vineyard explosion that started in 1882 catapulted Livermore to the front ranks of American wine regions.

The land rush was triggered by a report from Charles Wetmore to the state Viticultural Commission in 1883, favorably comparing the natural conditions of the Livermore Valley to some of the great wine regions of France. Taking his own advice, Wetmore had already purchased the Livermore land that became the Cresta Blanca winery in 1882, and he was soon joined by eager investors from near and far.

Like the Livermore Valley of today, dozens of small growers tried their hand at cultivating grapes. But the real buzz came from larger investors, men who had made money in some other line of business and approached the prospect of winemaking with ambitious plans. In 1882, Julius Paul Smith began planting vines and olive trees on a 2000-acre parcel at Olivina. In 1883, besides James Concannon's arrival from San Francisco, Carl Heinrich Wente came down from Napa and took over the George Bernard vineyard, and John Crellin purchased 450 acres in nearby Pleasanton to launch Ruby Hill. The next year, Louis Mel planted Le Bocage and began importing vines from France; Adrien Chaucé established Mont Rouge; and Alexander Duvall began work on Chateau Bellevue. Joseph Altschul came out from New York to plant the Vienna Vineyards in 1885, and longtime grower George True tripled his acreage in 1886.

By the mid-1890s, Livermore had well over than a hundred vineyards and more than 4000 acres under vine—a level not reached again until a full century later. Annual production suddenly totaled a million gallons of wine. Most of it was hearty reds made from Zinfandel and a mix of grapes from the Rhône, but it would be the whites that made the rising area's initial reputation. A white dessert wine from Wetmore's Cresta Blanca winery took the Grand Prize at an international exposition in Paris in 1889, and two other Livermore wines won Gold medals. It was the first time any wine from California had ever beaten the best of Europe—and almost a century before the famous "Judgment of Paris" tasting in 1976 at which wines from Napa bested their French counterparts.

The pace of expansion was dizzying, but quality was the hallmark. In 1893, Charles Bundschu of the state Viticultural Commission reflected on the decade just past and reported, "Alameda County, and especially Livermore Valley, appears to have made the most formidable progress in the general rivalry for the production of the higher types of fine table wine." An auspicious start for a new wine region.

Courtesy Of The Livermore Heritage Guild

DOWNTOWN LIVERMORE
1890

13

The Rocky Heart of Livermore

James Concannon picked a remarkable spot to plant his vines. The Concannon Vineyard, full of rocks and gravel, in places running hundreds of feet deep, can lay claim to being the signature soil of the Livermore Valley.

Some perspective on the Valley and the vineyard comes from people who know both well.

Sergio Traverso, winemaker at Concannon from 1981 to 1989, still consulting for Murrieta's Well in Livermore while making his own wines in Chile and Argentina:

> *The rocky soil of Livermore is a marvelous example of austerity. It has a large proportion of rocks of alluvial origin, with a predominance of quartz, a fact that makes it eternal. The proportion varies, but it is at its highest in a fan that comes from the southeast hillsides, passing through Wente's vineyard and then Concannon to end at the edge of the City of Livermore, providing a most precious substrata. The rest of the soil composition is a sandy loam. The effect on the grape quality is the same as any other rocky soil around the world: low water retention, excellent drainage and deep root penetration.*

> *The Livermore Valley is one of the very few California coastal valleys that is oriented west to east, rather than north to south. This fact allows for the maritime breeze coming from the ocean to travel in a direct line over the Bay, blowing into the Valley with the same punctuality as an English train. Day after day during the growing season, the Valley starts cool in the morning, and by 1:00 or 2:00, the temperature has reached its maximum. Hot air goes up, sucking in the cold air from the ocean, and then the breeze rushes in. Before sunset, the Valley is cooler than, say, St. Helena in the Napa Valley. The difference between the maximum and minimum is large, but the maximum does not last very long. The consequence is tremendous finesse in the wines.*

Tom Lane, Concannon winemaker from 1992 to 2003, now winemaker for Bianchi Vineyards in Paso Robles:

> *The rocks and gravel in the soil are distinctive, and the soils on the north side of Tesla Road are very consistent. They make for reduced vigor, so the vines can concentrate on putting flavors in the grapes rather than growing leaves. Soils that drain well can be fine-tuned with irrigation. During growing season, you can give it less or more water at crucial times—fruit set, veraision, cell division. If the soil holds a lot of water, there's not much ability to do that fine tuning.*

Phil Wente, Vice President and head of vineyard operations for Wente Vineyards, and a part-owner of Concannon Vineyard in the 1990s:

> *Everyone talks about the rocks and gravel of the Livermore Valley, but not everyone has those rocks and gravel. There's a belt of rocky soils, 500 yards on either side of both of the arroyos that run through the center of the Valley, and Concannon has, in what's north of Tesla, probably the most consistent 150 acres—gravel to pea gravel to small rock gravel. The consistency is the thing. We have bands of real rocky soil in our own vineyard, but then clay another 100 yards out. What's unique about the whole Concannon parcel is its uniformity, and that makes for great wine—all the vines perform equally, every berry ripens together.*

THE MEXICAN CONNECTION

Grandfather's venture into grapegrowing in Mexico is definitely one of the more interesting and colorful chapters in the Concannon story—although I'm afraid nobody living really knows much about it.

When he was in the rubber stamp business in the 1870s, before he established the winery, Grandfather's sales territory kept expanding and expanding, and eventually included Mexico. That was, among other things, a great incentive for him to learn Spanish. While he was down there, he saw an opportunity to open up a completely different business—organizing and improving the street-sweeping and rubbish collection in Mexico City. So he obtained a franchise from the government, ran the street-sweeping operation for a few years, and later sold it to a French engineering company. In the process, he had demonstrated his business skills to President Porfirio Diaz.

A few years later, as a way to raise capital for the vineyards in Livermore, Grandfather persuaded Diaz to let him help develop and expand Mexico's grape and wine industry. Their plan was to import cuttings of the better European grape varieties and plant them around the country. From 1889 to 1904, Grandfather shipped millions of grapevine cuttings from Livermore to Mexico, whole railroad cars full of them. It was a huge project. The shipments were big news in the local papers.

The cuttings went to a central distribution point in Celaya, in the state of Guanajuato, northwest of Mexico City, and from there were parceled out to all the great haciendas. According to the stories, Grandfather would personally show up at the haciendas escorted by government troops. He probably got introduced as Don Jaime Concannon. You could take this grand military entrance a couple ways: as a sign of the undertaking's prestige or as some pretty serious arm-twisting by Diaz. Grandfather spent a lot of time personally supervising the plantings, and eventually brought in one of his brothers from Ireland to help out.

Not long afterwards, the Mexican Revolution broke out, and that was it for Diaz. The whole hacienda system went into chaos, and that ended the Concannon connection once and for all. Our family lost touch with that whole venture and with Mexican winemaking. As I understand it, most of those vines probably just died of neglect.

Still, the whole effort does show how people in Livermore, people like my grandfather, thought big in those days. If they were going to get into the wine business, they were really going to get into the wine business.

Concannon Grapes and Mexican Wine

The project James Concannon and President Porfirio Diaz envisioned—sending carloads of grapevines to Mexico to create a modern wine industry—wasn't as crazy an idea as it might seem. Mexico, in fact, has been producing wine longer than anywhere in the Americas, and boasts the oldest winery in the hemisphere—Casa Madero, founded in 1597. And it was the Mission Fathers from Mexico—then part of Spain—who first planted wine grapes up and down the California coast and proved there was the potential for successful winemaking.

Shortly after conquering the Aztecs in 1521, Hernán Cortés encouraged the development of winegrowing by requiring those who received land grants in New Spain to plant 1,000 vines a year for five years. By the end of the next century, New Spain's wine production was of sufficient quantity and quality that it was putting a dent in Old Spain's wine trade, so the Spanish Crown banned it entirely in 1699, leaving an exception only for the Missions. The ban on grapes and wine was one of the grievances that eventually fueled sentiment for independence, and was a particular irritant for Father Miguel Hidalgo, the firebrand priest who initiated the 11-year struggle that won Mexico its independence in 1821. So in a sense, the restrictions on wine grapes were for Mexico what the duties on tea were for the Bostonians who threw the Tea Party.

Mexico had a small number of commercial wineries in operation, both in the mainland states and on the Baja California peninsula, when Diaz and James Concannon launched their ambitious plan. For the most part, the cuttings didn't go to the existing wineries, but to the large haciendas, which had no tradition of grapegrowing and were often not situated in the most hospitable climates for wine grapes. Chances are that both Diaz and Concannon were keener on the whole idea than the haciendados.

When the Mexican Revolution came in 1910, sending Diaz into exile in 1911, the haciendas were the prime target of all the forces demanding land reform and a more equitable distribution of wealth. Turmoil was everywhere, properties were sacked, and nobody could be expected to worry about tending grapevines. When much of the hacienda land was later turned over to agricultural cooperatives, peasant farmers replanted with the crops they knew best.

Today, many people in the wine industry in Mexico are aware of the Diaz-Concannon story, but those efforts are more like a legend than a direct link to the contemporary scene. In the past few decades, Mexican producers—primarily in the Guadalupe Valley region near Ensenada in Baja California but also in the states of Sonora, Zacatecas, Querétaro and Coahuila—have finally broken into the world wine market and onto fine restaurant wine lists, north and south of the border.

James Concannon had a more lasting impact on the future of the Livermore Valley than on the vineyards of Mexico. But he likely has the distinction of being the first US citizen to plant grapes in both Californias—Baja and Alta.

OVERCOMING HARD TIMES

Prohibition was a miserable period for the wine business, and the Depression years were miserable for everybody in the country, but our little winery came through it all in pretty good shape. Because we had been making altar wine for 35 years, we stayed in business, perfectly legal, and never missed a harvest. So it turned out that Archbishop Alemany's advice, and Grandfather's decision to give it a try, were smarter than anyone knew at the time.

These were the years when my father, Joseph Concannon, headed up the winery. My grandfather, who was basically self-educated, encouraged all his sons to go to college and get an education, My dad chose a military career instead. He went into the First Cavalry—which really was, back in those days, a cavalry, soldiers on horseback. He got involved in the operations along the border during the time of the Mexican Revolution, serving under General John Pershing and Lieutenant George Patton. He would have been happy to stay in the military—except that Grandmother made him come back and take over the winery when it fell on hard times in the years after Grandfather died in 1911.

That military connection was always part of Dad's life, even when the winery was his main job. On the eve of World War I, he had two Concannon stained-glass windows donated to Saint Michael's, our local Catholic church, one in remembrance of his father, James Concannon, and one simply initialed "JSC." A few years later, he was promoted to captain in the Reserves, and from then on, he was known as Captain Joe. He wore khakis around the winery every day for fifty years. He would send General Pershing a case of wine every year. We have thank-you notes from 1939 and 1940.

Undoubtedly one reason he rose so fast in the cavalry was that he was already a fine horseman. As a young man, he used to ride from Livermore to Yosemite. He was one of the founders of the Livermore Rodeo in 1918—and it's still around today. He always used to tell the story about how he bought my older sister Marie a pony from the circus, and the pony kind of had a mind of its own. One day my father came across Marie on the pony, which was headed the wrong way, back into town looking for the circus, and Marie couldn't control him. So my dad rode up alongside them, scooped her off the horse—and sold the pony back to the circus.

By the time my dad went to work at the winery, Prohibition was already on the horizon. Anti-alcohol sentiment had been building for years, and both my grandfather and my father had been active locally in campaigning against it. When Prohibition went into effect in 1920, it was a blow to us, but at least we were able to keep making wine for the church.

Altar wine, or sacramental wine, isn't that much different from ordinary wine. The main things the church looked for were, first, that the wine had to be made entirely from natural grape products, including any brandy or spirits used to fortify the wine; and second, the wine had to be sound—the church felt that if the wine was spoiled, turning to vinegar or something like that, then the Mass wasn't valid. A lot of it really had to do with the character of the people making the wine; the bishops who certified the wine for sacramental use wanted to be sure the winery was on the up and up, honest, clean, not pulling any fast ones. We passed the test.

In that period, we had three basic wine styles. The lead wine was Angelica, basically a white port, made from French Colombard and a mix of other white grapes, fortified with grape brandy to 18% alcohol, and aged four years in wood—a wonderful wine. Then there was a Muscat de Frontignan, also fortified; and the Chateau Concannon, a Sauternes-style sweet wine where we stopped the fermentation, ending up with about 12% alcohol and 3% sugar. Because of the high alcohol, the fortified wines were very stable in the bottle or the barrel, which was important because we shipped them all over the world—China, the Philippines, Rome.

Producing altar wine meant my dad could keep the operation running, keep the equipment working, and maintain some kind of distribution network, even if it was limited. There were only about half a dozen wineries in northern California that stayed open making sacramental wine, and it definitely helped keep our name and the reputation alive. Years later, I would meet former altar boys who were introduced to Concannon wine because that's what the priests had around. And we were selling wine not just to the Catholic church, but to Lutherans and Episcopalians and others as well.

Even though the winery was still in production, it didn't generate a lot of income, and with Prohibition showing no signs of going away, prospects didn't look good. My dad's brothers and sisters weren't interested in trying to keep it going, so he had to figure out a way to refinance the business. It wasn't easy finding money for a winery in the middle of Prohibition, but fortunately, he found a solution.

My mother, Giovanina Ferrario, came to Livermore from Lonate Pozzolo, Italy, north of Milano, in her early twenties. She lived with her older brother, Carlo Ferrario, who also had a local winery. It was through Carlo and Dad's common interest in wine that he met my mother. They were married in 1925 at Saint Michael's Church, and their wedding reception was held at what is now Ravenswood in Livermore. Uncle Carlo loaned Dad the money, which he later paid back, so that he could purchase the interests of his brothers and sisters. He and his wife Nina were now the sole proprietors of the winery.

Dad did bring in two of his brothers to work at the winery—Robert to handle sales and Tom to do the winemaking. Uncle Tom had been trained as a chemist, so he brought a lot of technical knowledge to the winemaking process, unusual for those days. Combining the altar wine and running cattle and various other side projects, my dad somehow did well enough during Prohibition to pay some of the best artisans in San Francisco to build the front gate, with all that brick and iron work, in 1929. It made quite a statement that we were still going strong.

CONCANNON VINEYARDS SACRAMENTAL WINES

WINE BLESSED BY REDEMPTIONIST FATHERS AND SENT TO POPE PIUS XIII
1936

First in Seattle Since Prohibition
CARLOAD of FINE WINES
Shipped By
CONCANNON VINEYARDS
From Livermore, Cal.
to
U.S. Govt. Bonded Warehouse—Seattle
F. M. FAIRBANKS Winery Agent

DON'T OPEN UNTIL — Here's Seattle's first real wine shipment, greeted by a group of pretty usherettes from the Roxy Theatre. | The wine was shipped by the famous Concannon Vineyards and consigned to F. H Fairbanks, Northwest agent for the company

SEATTLE POST-INTELLIGENCER
1933

CAPTAIN JOSEPH CONCANNON
1918

When Repeal finally came along in 1933, we had plenty of wine in tanks ready to go. Dad put up a circus tent on the lawn out in front of the winery and hired a hundred men to help with the bottling and labeling. There was a line of trucks that stretched halfway into town hauling the wine away, taking it to the railroad and shipping it by train all over the country. The thing that got the most publicity of all was that Dad sent a boatload of wine to Seattle; and when it arrived, there was a big celebration, with banners saying, "Welcome Concannon" and a lot of press coverage.

Coming out of Prohibition, Concannon was a pretty strong brand in the 1930s. It was on fancy restaurant wine lists, not just in San Francisco, but on the East Coast. We were shipping wine in barrels to missionaries in China. My dad sent a barrel of wine every year to the Pope, and of course that got picked up by the papers. After Repeal, my uncle Robert got Concannon wines placed in railroad dining cars all over the country—very visible. It wasn't a big winery, and didn't have the money for huge advertising campaigns, but I think my dad had a flair for getting the wine and the winery noticed.

In 1939, as the Depression was ending and war was looming, my dad put up a new flagpole, along the driveway leading up to the house from Tesla Road. He had a local blacksmith make it out of several lengths of steel pipe, and then arranged for a crew from the utility company to come out and assemble it and hoist it up. In the cement base, along with the date, he recognized the workers who put it up, and also included the names of two Army recruiters he had worked with in the years after he left the active military. That kind of thing was typical of my dad—make sure to give other people credit.

The dedication of the flagpole was a big local event—Dad invited the whole town, had a band, a detachment of servicemen, did it up right. Dad raised that flag himself every day, up till shortly before he died, and then I took over the job for several years. When I drive into the winery today, the first thing I do is check and make sure the flag is up.

The Paradox of Prohibition

From a distance of seven decades, the era of Prohibition seems like one big blank spot in the history of winemaking in America. But in fact those 13 dry years were a jumble of contradictions, some built into the law itself, some the result of widespread public opposition, and some demonstrating the ingenuity of winemakers under trying circumstances.

When the 18th Amendment to the Constitution was formally ratified and the enabling legislation—the Volstead Act—went into effect on January 29, 1920, the wine business, like the rest of the alcoholic beverage industry, suffered a severe contraction. In 1922, there were still 919 bonded wineries in the United States, 694 of them in California, all hoping Prohibition would blow over quickly; by 1933, just before Repeal became real, the numbers had dwindled to 268 for the country and 177 for the state, most of them not really functioning. Seeing little future in its existing training programs, the University of California Department of Viticulture and Enology changed its name to Viticulture and Fruit Products.

But the law was full of loopholes, which, over time, were fully exploited. The manufacture, sale and export of intoxicating beverages were all prohibited—but not their purchase, possession or consumption. Winemaking for non-beverage purposes was allowed—including sacramental wine, medicinal use and the distillation of industrial alcohol—all of which turned out to be very popular product lines indeed.

Only a handful of California wineries kept their operations intact by focusing on altar wines—Concannon in Livermore, Beaulieu Vineyards in St. Helena, Novitiate in Los Gatos, the Christian Brothers in Martinez, San Antonio Winery in Los Angeles among them. A number

of other wineries managed to get a small piece of the altar wine market. Others made wine for use in flavoring food products, or supplied the ever-expanding field of medical tonics. Since the authorities didn't want to seem anti-farmer, growers were often able to obtain permission to turn their grapes into wine, for lack of any alternative use; but with no outlet, tens of millions of gallons of wine stored in tanks eventually went bad.

The biggest surprise was the unquenchable thirst for grapes among home winemakers, especially in the eastern US. The Volstead Act allowed families to make up to 200 gallons of wine a year for personal consumption, which was deemed a "non-intoxicating" use. Suddenly, a nation of home winemakers sprung up, clamoring for both fresh grapes and grape juice concentrate—the latter often carrying stern warnings that if by some chance water and yeast were added to the contents, wine could result.

By 1927, 72,000 railroad carloads of grapes were shipped east annually. Amazingly, planted vineyard acreage in California nearly doubled, from 300,000 acres in 1920 to 577,000 in 1927, a level not reached again until the 1970s. Over-planting inevitably led to a crash in the late 1920s, but in the meantime, total wine production in the country probably doubled, thanks to eager amateurs.

Overall, Prohibition took its toll. Most winemaking facilities were torn down or left to deteriorate; skilled personnel left the business in droves and no replacements were trained. Vineyard acreage was planted to varieties that shipped well, but didn't necessarily make for quality wines. All of which meant that when Repeal came in December 1933, wineries like Concannon that had stayed in business offering altar wines were the undisputed industry leaders.

REVIVAL AND RECOGNITION

World War II wasn't the greatest time to be in the wine business. For one thing, there was a severe shortage of agricultural labor. Field workers were almost non-existent. In 1943, with harvest time approaching and no workers in sight, Dad talked with the commanding officer at the local Naval Air Station—it was where the Lawrence Livermore Laboratories are now—and got his approval to bring some of the seamen stationed there over as pickers. These fellows from Oklahoma and Manhattan who hadn't ever seen a grapevine in their lives harvested grapes for two weeks, and Dad made sure the seamen got paid for their work. We have a picture of a couple dozen sailors in the field in their work clothes and white hats. How many people can say they had the Navy save a crop?

Another time during the war, two of the biplanes used for training at the naval base collided and crashed out behind the winery, killing three pilots and devastating part of the vineyard. Some time later, a representative from the Navy came out to make a settlement for the cost of the damage. Dad said to him, "Give me those papers and let me sign off. I don't want any payment. Those young men's lives were so much more important than any material thing you could give me."

Right after the war ended, just as things were returning to normal, my Uncle Robert Concannon died. He had been responsible for handling the winery's sales. The next year, my Uncle Tom, the winemaker, passed away. That left my dad all by himself, responsible for every part of the operation. He didn't have the technical background Tom had or the marketing experience Bob had, so losing both of them at an early age was a real setback. But somehow my dad kept things together.

It helped that he was such a friendly, gregarious Irishman who could relate to all kinds of people. He could put on a suit or wear khakis; he could talk to the seamen and the admirals. He didn't have an enemy in the world. He was humble, and he had a sense of humor. Frequently when visitors came to the winery, he would meet them in his casual work clothes and claim to be the caretaker, or maybe just "Mr. Smith." Only after he'd shown them around, tasted some wine, and checked out what kind of people they were, would he admit, "I'm Joseph S. Concannon."

Even without any formal business training, he had a good sense of how to solve problems, get things done and promote our wine. When he sent a barrel of wine to the Pope every year, it was because he was a good Catholic. But it also got us some press. He managed to maintain the tradition and get the wine to the Vatican during World War II, even though we were at war with Italy. My Dad received a papal medal from Pope John XXIII. I guess he must have liked our wine.

Or shipping wine to China. I can remember as a kid going down with him to the docks in San Francisco. This was the era when there was a big effort to unionize the longshoremen, and it could be hard to keep cargo moving and not have it held up because of some dispute. My dad would walk up to the lead guy on the docks and hand him a bottle of wine. We were always able to get our shipments through.

Dad knew that, with his brothers gone, he needed help in the winery. So in 1950, he hired Katherine Vajda, who was working over at Cresta Blanca, to take charge of the winemaking at Concannon. As near as I can tell, that made her the first woman winemaker in California, at least the first one with real technical training. For years, she was on the Wine Institute's Technical Advisory Committee—24 men and Katherine. She was a tough taskmaster and trained me for the job before I took over in 1960.

My dad made sure that our winery out in Livermore played an active role in the California wine industry. He was involved with the Wine Institute from the time it was founded in 1934 and a director for many years. Most of the wineries that built the Wine Institute were family-owned, and the Concannons were one of them, on a first-name basis with the Martinis and the Sebastianis and so on, working with them to improve the quality of wine and promote the industry.

My dad was friends with Georges de Latour and Andre Tchelistcheff, and the family used to go up to Beaulieu Vineyards to visit them when I was a kid. I remember Tchelistcheff showing us around the place; we were in awe of him, of course, even though we lived at a winery and knew what went on there. He always credited Dad with coming up with his favorite description for the aromas of great Pinot Noir—rose petals that have been in the glass for a couple days.

JOSEPH SR. ON HORSEBACK, JOE & JIM STANDING ON TRACTOR
1936

STOWING IN SHIPS BOUND FOR CHINA MISSIONARIES
1941

I remember one day when August Sebastiani dropped by the winery. I saw this guy sitting in the office and thought he was the janitor, but it turned out to be August, in his usual straw hat and horn-rimmed glasses and coveralls. He was on his way to a fishing trip in the Sacramento Delta and just wanted to stop by for coffee and to see how the Concannon boys were doing.

My parents were Irish and Italian, and the Martinis of course were all-Italian. Louis Martini, Sr., would come by periodically, in the limo he went around in during those days, and that would give Mother a chance to speak Italian, which she greatly enjoyed. I remember the time he shipped her a couple cases of his 1946 Reserve Cabernet. One day she heard Dad and someone shouting out in front of the winery office, and when she asked what the argument had been about, Dad said, "No argument, that was just me and Louis Martini discussing wine." I guess they both had pretty loud voices.

When visitors from the other wine families came by, or celebrities dropped in, or Dad brought people home, Mom would scramble to put a meal together. She always did a good job. One time in the late 1950s, Queen Frederika of Greece showed up on about half an hour's notice. She had been visiting the Lawrence Livermore labs, and her plans for the afternoon fell through. So she decided to come to the winery. Dad came into the house and said to Mother, "The Queen of Greece is coming by, so I'm going to put on a suit." She thought he was kidding, but then he walked out in his suit. She put on her best blue dress, and everything was ready when the Queen arrived. The Secret Service officer had a little camera; I still have the picture of Mom, Dad, me and the queen.

In the 1950s, there still weren't a lot of wineries open for visiting. Even though we didn't have a tasting room with regular hours, people knew Dad would welcome them and show them

around. The crooner Rudy Vallee used to come by in his fancy Rolls Royce every year, usually with a new wife. Apparently, he was into wine. Once he tore his jacket, and Dad brought him to the house—as usual, with no notice—for Mom to do some mending. He sent us some records, but since they were kind of risqué, Mother made us destroy them all.

Dennis Day, the singer and actor, was another visitor. One time Dad was in a generous mood and gave him a bunch of gift boxes, and Dennis said, "I'll take it, but you have to tell me what the charge is and bill me." That's the kind of guy he was.

The celebrities made for good stories, but I think the day that meant the most to my dad was in 1958, when the plaque designating the winery as California Historical Landmark number 641 was dedicated. All the county supervisors were there, along with Joseph Knowland, publisher of the Oakland Tribune and a priest, of course. Best of all, Chief Justice Earl Warren came out for the day. Warren knew Dad from years earlier, when he served as District Attorney for Alameda County, before he became Governor of California. There was a lunch in what is now the tasting room. It was a very special day for Dad, and wonderful recognition for the winery and its traditions.

A lot of Livermore and many people from the wine world turned out for my father's memorial and funeral when he died in 1965. He had been active in the local community—he served on the high school board, just as my grandfather had—and was a well-known figure in the industry. By the time he died, Joe and I were already running the winery; but seeing all those people who came to the funeral to pay their respects really showed us what our father had left us.

ELLEN CONCANNON
1849-1922

NINA FERRARIO CONCANNON
1899-1972

The Concannon Women

The history of the Concannon Vineyard can be marked off into eras defined by the men who were in charge: founder James Concannon; his son Joseph (Captain Joe), working with his brothers, Robert and Thomas; and the third generation, Captain Joe's sons Joe and Jim. But in a winery so strongly identified with a close-knit family, the men are only half the story. Three of the Concannon women, Helen, Jim's wife, Peggy, Joe's widow, and Nina Concannon Radisch, younger sister of Jim and Joe, shed light on the women who came before and their own roles in the winery.

On Ellen Rowe Concannon:

Helen: Grandmother came from Castle Comer, Kilkenny County, Ireland. Very little has been written about her, but she must have been an extraordinary woman to have raised such a large family (five boys and five girls) and taken care of a newly established business and vineyard while her husband traveled extensively.

Nina: I wish I had known my grandmother. Here's the reality: after my grandparents moved to Livermore, my grandfather went to France, all the way around Cape Horn, to get grapevines and learn about winemaking. It must have taken him months to do that, and it left my grandmother in charge. Then he went off to Mexico, first to run the sanitation business, then to distribute grapevines and introduce viticulture. So who ran the place? Women rise to the occasion.

On Giovanina (Nina) Ferrario Concannon:

Peggy: The wine business was a very male-run industry. At Concannon, Nina was always part of the winery and involved in the decisions. But then, it wasn't so much that the family owned the winery—the winery was part of their family. It was all very integrated, especially with the family house at the winery. She was a woman of few words, but when she spoke, you listened.

Helen: Nina was very kind and helpful to me as a young bride and mother. We had a good relationship, in part because I had come from the Midwest to a community where I knew no one, as she had done, coming from Italy. She had been the new girl in town, too. It was much the same when I met and married Jim—there was a lot of catching up to do, and she was a real friend and helpmate in those times. As a mother-in-law, she was wonderful, and a special grandmother to the children.

Nina: When my mother first came over from Italy, she planned just to visit for a while with her brother Carlo and then return. But she had gotten sick on the voyage over and couldn't bear to go back. After some time here, she met my dad. She was starting to learn English, and thought it would be prudent to learn more. She arranged to be a volunteer with the first grade at our local Catholic school, Saint Michael's; she helped with the children, and it helped her with her English while she was at it. She ended up speaking perfect, beautiful English.

My parents followed traditional male and female roles. At Thanksgiving or Christmas or whatever the holiday was, the women went into the kitchen and did all the dishes and the men walked around the winery smoking cigars, because my mother would not allow smoking in the house. But on normal days, my father always dried the dishes for my mother. It was their time together, a time to talk just on a one-to-one basis, to joke, to talk about the business, to talk about us.

Peggy: One little thing I remember is that egg whites were often used at the winery to clarify the wine. Nina wouldn't dream of throwing them out; instead, she made the most terrific sponge cake.

On Tastings and Entertaining:

Peggy: In the late 1950s and the 1960s, the wine industry was just getting started, and everybody was in the same boat. Wine tastings were a way for charities to raise money, and we would do almost anything to get wine out there before the public. San Francisco, Oakland, Alameda, Los Angeles—wherever anybody wanted us, we'd go. There weren't that many people in the industry in those days, mostly families—the Mirassous, the Mondavis, the Wentes, the Martinis—and we often traveled around as a group. Even Bob Mondavi would haul his two cases of wine on the bus to LA; nobody could afford to fly in those days. At the nearby tastings, we would have bread and cheese at our table. The cheese came from a wonderful local cheese factory in Pleasanton, huge wheels of Jack, and I remember sitting at the table in our house on P Street in Livermore cutting little squares of cheese until midnight.

Helen: The tasting events in the '60s and into the early '70s were a popular way to introduce people to California wine. Most of the wineries that attended had their family name on the bottle, and it was a time for us to visit with other wine families as well as advertise and educate people about wine. Holding events at the winery came later, starting in the mid-'70s. Concannon started Art in the Vineyard, a two-day event where local artists displayed and sold their work and guests could enjoy the grounds and taste wine. Our children and their cousins were always busy with the wine glass brigade.

When special guests would visit the winery, they would often come by the house, and it was not unusual for them to stay for lunch or dinner. People entertained more frequently in their homes in those days, rather then dining out. When it was a wine writer or a food critic, I was always relieved to find out who it was only after the fact.

JIM AND JOE

When my brother Joe and I and our sisters were growing up, it was a fairly simple life. There wasn't a lot of pressure to get into the wine business; the main thing was to learn our numbers, read the classics, and get an education. We went to St. Michael's grade school and then to Livermore High. Joe and I would come home from school and be in the great outdoors. The Arroyo Mocho creek was only a couple hundred yards from the house, and that was a great place for little guys to go and not get in trouble. We could catch frogs and turtles and look for fish and adventures.

We always had some chores to do around the winery. I remember picking up rocks from the vineyard from the time I was very young, but my first real job was carrying water out to the grape pickers. There were whole families out there. Grape-picking was one of the mainstays of employment in Livermore during the Depression.

My dad installed a siren on top of the winery—before that, Grandfather had a bell—and it would sound every day to signal to the workers and the family when it was time for lunch and when the workday was over. There was a control button in our house, and it happened to be very close to the light switch near the bathroom. More times than I can count, visitors would hit the wrong switch and set off the siren. The guests would be scared half to death, but the kids always got a laugh out of it.

I got used to having wine at the family table. The idea of letting the children have a little ration of wine was brought into the family by my mother, from the Italian side. We had little glasses, about the size of shot glasses. Not on every day, but at least a couple of times a week, we could have wine—starting when we were maybe six or seven. If we messed up, we didn't get our ration, so we were sure to be in good graces with Mom during dinner. It was a tradition we had and I still have those glasses.

Mom was also the one who gave the final blessing to a new wine or a new blend. She didn't drink a lot of wine, but she had a very good, sensitive palate, and Dad or Uncle Tom would always run things by her. And it wasn't just a courtesy. If she thought the wine was off or needed something, they'd go back into the winery and work on it. I used to do the same thing with my wife Helen later on.

I was about ten when I made my first wine. I got hold of some grape juice and some yeast and put it in a bottle, and hid it up in the attic—where the old water tank house had been, right above my parents' bedroom. Naturally it started to ferment and foamed over the top and leaked down through the floor and ceiling into the bedroom. My dad figured out pretty quickly that his son had tried to make wine and had screwed up. So he said, "If you're thinking of doing this, why don't you work with Uncle Tom?"

And I did. I started cleaning the lab, washing out tanks, washing bottles. During World War II, we had to use second-hand bottles—we'd call it recycling today—and we'd wash them a second time when we got them, a simple task for a little guy like me. I remember that we had 126 wooden tanks in those days, and I probably spent time cleaning out every one of them. Working with Uncle Tom got me used to being around winemaking and gave me the bug to eventually become more serious.

What I grew up with was old-time winemaking, with a lot of manual labor and improvisation. We filled our bottles by hand—some continued to get done that way until about 1980—and we used a basket press until we retired it in the 1970s. You can still see the tracks where the cake of pressed grape skins was rolled out of the winery—it took five men to haul the load of skins through the door. To circulate the red wine and the floating cap of skins in our big redwood tanks during fermentation, we would drain the wine into a sump below the floor level, then pump it back in at the top of the tank—a primitive form of the "pump-over" done in today's stainless steel wine tanks.

In the eighth grade, I won a prize for being at the top of the class in science—the prize was a chemistry book I still have. But in college at St. Mary's I studied business and accounting, not chemistry. When I graduated in 1953, I went into the Army. This was during the Korean War. Right after I completed basic training, the armistice was declared, so I spent my entire two-year hitch at Fort Ord down near Monterey as a clerk/typist.

Joe, who was three years older than I, had gone to Notre Dame for college and then served in the military. Then he started working at the winery, doing sales. One day when I had a month or two left to go in the service, he dropped by to visit me at Ford Ord, while he was in the area selling wine out of the back of his car. He proposed that I should come to work at the winery, too. We could split things up and be a tremendous team. The day after I got out, I came back to the winery. From then on, Joe handled the vineyards and the sales, and I gradually took over the winemaking.

Having grown up around the winery, I knew the physical setup, but there was a lot of technical knowledge I didn't have. I learned a lot from Katherine Vajda, our winemaker at the time. She was a tough taskmaster. If I missed a chemical analysis by five parts per million, I'd have to run it over again till I could run four or five tests at once and get them all right. She slowly guided me into the work. I took over as head winemaker in 1960 at the very same time I married my wife Helen. Taking on a new job and a family all at once was a lot. I remember when Katherine and I walked out the door together for the last time, she said, "Jimmy, you can do it." I thought, "Wow, I'm really in trouble!" But it turned out OK.

I took short courses up at Davis, including some three-week summer classes for winery personnel. They were intense—all the latest information, from the great Davis professors of that era—Maynard Amerine, Vernon Singleton, Cornelius Ough. The people in the classes were from wineries all over California, and also included a lot of the founders of the wine industries in Oregon and Washington.

Nothing was automated the way winery facilities often are now. Way back, before we had any refrigeration, we would cool down the tanks of fermenting white wine by dropping 250-pound blocks of dry ice into a vat of water, then circulating the wine through the cold water with a metal coil, trying to get it down to 50 degrees. Even with a heat exchanger acquired in the 1960s, we had to cool the wine down one tank at a time, which meant we were playing catch-up all day and all night. Then there was the Zinfandel Rosé; you had to press the juice off the skins at just the right time to get the proper color, and somehow that always turned out to be at two in the morning.

During harvest time, I would sleep on an Army cot in the winery. That was the only way to get things done. I always said it's like a doctor delivering a baby. If it happens in the middle of the night, that's when you have to do it.

JIM CONCANNON
1957

CAPTAIN JOE, JIM, AND JOSEPH JR. CONCANNON
1959

The most famous picture to come out of the Concannon wine cellars is probably the shot of me sticking my head through the door of a tank. It was taken by a professional photographer, and the Wine Institute used it for public relations purposes for years. After I did the pose, he got a little carried away and decided to take some more shots from inside the tank. I was in my late 20s and fairly skinny and knew my way around a wine tank. He was built a little different, and got stuck. We finally helped pull him out, and he said, "You'll get copies of this photograph, but I'm never coming back to this winery again!"

Even operating on a shoestring, we never knocked down the quality of the wine. In the era when I was winemaker the major challenge for the California wine industry was to make clean, sound, reliable wine, because there had been a lot of really inferior wine on the market. And we did that; we never bottled wine that was off, and never had shipments of wine go bad in the bottle.

Joe was really careful about our grape sources beyond our own vineyard. We didn't want to expand production by blending down with lesser grapes. He would scour vineyards in Sonoma and Mendocino, and, for a while, we got some excellent grapes from the Santa Cruz mountains. Chaffee Hall, an attorney from San Francisco, had founded Hallcrest Vineyards down there in the 1940s and had made some of California's best Cabernets and White Rieslings. When he decided to retire, he asked Joe to take over the vineyard. He knew Joe would treat it right.

Joe was always involved with the viticulture program at UC Davis, working with the faculty and experimenters there, trying out new grapes in field tests and sending plant material to Davis for them to study and propagate. It's no surprise that when he died, all the top viticulturalists from Davis and the USDA came to pay their respects. He and I were both active with the Wine Institute, keeping on top of technical issues and serving on the board of directors.

There was always something to do at the winery, and I didn't get a chance to travel around much. But I remember one time we went down to Palm Springs for a Wine Institute board meeting, and, after the meeting, Helen and I went out with Joe Heitz, Jack Davies of Schramsberg, Chuck Carpy of Freemark Abbey and their wives. We let Joe Heitz order the wine, and the first thing he did was complain that the restaurant was charging too much for Heitz wine. This was a while back, and they were charging $20. Then he ordered a bottle of Schramsberg sparkling wine, and it was flat. But we had a great night, and drank a lot of Heitz's wines, and Jack Davies played the piano, and we closed the place up at 2 o'clock. Nights like that were very special.

We were always proud of what our family had built up over the years. In 1975, I got a call from an office of Alameda County, saying that the old Concannon Vineyard gate would have to come down, because it violated some signage ordinance. I thought to myself, "It's only been there 50 years." I went down to the County offices and found the person in charge. He came out the next day, we signed a waiver, I paid a $25 fee, and that was that. We weren't about to take down that gate.

THE 1989 CELEBRATION OF THE CONCANNON MILLENNIUM OF NAME (1000 YEARS) RECOGNIZED IN GALWAY IRELAND

ELIZABETH AND LOUIE MARTINI (standing)
SERGIO AND MERCEDES TRAVERSO

JOHN DELUCA, JOE HEITZ, JIM CONCANNON AND LOU GOMBERG

DOROTHY AND ANDRE TCHELISTCHEFF

Katherine Vajda

Among the "firsts" on which Concannon prides itself is hiring Katherine Vajda (VIE-da), who can lay claim to have been the first technically-trained woman winemaker hired in California. Vajda's story has received relatively little attention in the standard versions of California wine history, in part because the term "winemaker" has so many definitions.

The chronicle of women in the wine industry starts in 1886, when Josephine Tychson took over the vineyards she and her husband John had planted near St. Helena in the Napa Valley (now the site of Freemark Abbey). After his early death, she proceeded to build a winery and produce wine for several years. In the same era, Isabel Simi Haigh took over Simi, her family's Sonoma winery, after her father's death, and actress Lily Langtry purchased land in the Guenoc Valley and brought in a French winemaker in a quest to make great wine.

Many of these early women wine pioneers were winery owners; some actually got their hands stained with grapes. But like most of the men of this era in California winemaking, their preparation was likely a brief apprenticeship, not a formal training in chemistry, biology and enology—the scientific background common among today's commercial winemakers. It was several decades before university-trained women enologists came on the scene—starting with MaryAnn Graf, the first female graduate of the University of California at Davis enology program in 1965. In 1973, she was named head winemaker at Simi. Zelma Long and Merry Edwards were among the other early Davis-trained women who went on to make their marks in the industry.

KATHERINE VAJDA, WINEMAKER
1950 -1960

But before that credentialed wave, in the 1950s, there was Katherine Vajda at Concannon. She was born in Hungary, studied dance and was a ballerina in Budapest when she married Julius Vajda, son of a business family. When fascism overtook Hungary, they fled to New York, and Julius eventually found an accounting job with the Cresta Blanca Winery in Livermore, owned at that time by Schenley Distillers.

Katherine, with no formal background, got a job as a lab technician and worked her way up. Cresta Blanca in those days was making, for the most part, generic, undistinguished wines, but it was still a high-powered operation with a solid technical staff. Among Vajda's mentors in her on-the-job training was Dr. Edmund Twight, a highly respected European-born authority on wine responsible over the years for significant improvements in the overall standards of California winemaking.

After the death of winemaker Tom Concannon in 1945, Concannon Vineyard's cellar team needed bolstering. Captain Joe Concannon and his son, Joe Jr., persuaded Katherine to leave Cresta Blanca and hired her to take over the winemaking at Concannon. From 1950 through 1960, when Jim Concannon became winemaker, Vajda handled the laboratory analysis and oversaw production, introducing among other things a very popular Riesling wine marketed as Moselle. In the 1950s, she was also an active participant in the Wine Institute's technical advisory work.

When Katherine left in 1960, she launched yet another career. After ballerina and winemaker, she turned interior decorator, and went on to considerable success in that field, too.

So when you celebrate the role of women in California wine, and toast the names of Josephine Tychson and MaryAnn Graf, remember to raise a glass to Katherine Vajda.

Concannon Clones and California Cabernet

Petite Sirah is the variety Concannon is best known for, starting with its first-ever release in 1964. But at about the same time, the vineyard made another contribution to the California wine industry and California wine history. This time, the grape was Cabernet Sauvignon.

Starting in 1959, Dr. Austin Goheen and Dr. Harold Olmo at the University of California at Davis, working with the wine industry, initiated a program to produce certified grapevine stock, selected for quality and productivity and treated (mainly with prolonged heat) to remove the viruses that afflicted so many vineyards.

In 1966, with the help of Joe Concannon, Goheen took Cabernet Sauvignon cuttings from the Concannon vineyard and put them into the cleanup and testing program. Records at Davis indicate all the samples came from a single vine—row 34, vine 2, of the Concannon Cabernet block. Based on different heat treatments, Davis eventually released Cabernet clones 7, 8 and 11 to the industry—known as the Concannon clones.

With relatively few certified strains of Cabernet on the market, nurseries and vineyard managers enthusiastically embraced the new Concannon clones, particularly 7 and 8. There's no way to reconstruct the number of acres planted to specific clones, but a consensus of old-timers—agricultural extension specialists, vine nurserymen, winery owners—agrees that the Concannon clones provided the backbone of the huge expansion in Cabernet Sauvignon plantings in the 1970s and '80s. Napa Valley Cabernet, the wine that more than any other put California on the world wine map in this era, was built on these vines.

In the 1990s, most of California's premium wine regions were forced to replant because of infestations of the phylloxera root louse. Once again, on new rootstock, clones 7 and 8 with their proven track records were popular choices, along with a spice rack of newer imports from France.

Wine industry insiders know about the Concannon Cabernet clones, but few consumers do. Concannon's own Cabernets have a loyal following, but the Concannon clones make good wine all over the state. So the next time you pop the cork on one of those $100-a-bottle ultra-premium Cabernets from a prime North Coast label, remember there's almost bound to be a piece of row 34, vine 2 in your glass.

Rkatsiteli and the Cold War

One of the most unusual projects Joe Concannon undertook in collaboration with the viticulturalists at UC Davis was growing Rkatsiteli (ur-COT-si-TEL-ee). The most widely planted white grape in Russia and all of eastern Europe for centuries, Rkatsiteli made its way to Davis through one of Dr. Harold Olmo's world-wide grape-hunting trips. Joe Concannon volunteered to try it out at the Concannon Vineyard in the 1970s. (Meanwhile, unknown to the Concannons, Dr. Konstantin Frank was already experimenting with Rkatsiteli in the Finger Lakes region of upstate New York at his Vinifera Cellars.)

Winemaker Jim Concannon had his doubts about his brother's new project. The grapes had large bunches and large berries, high acidity and high alcohol, and a very distinctive aromatic profile. The wine was too aggressive to blend into anything else and probably too obscure to market on its own. Jim remembers asking, "Why, in the middle of the Cold War, are we growing a Russian grape?" Bravely, Concannon released the wine with a double label, proclaiming the grape in both Anglicized letters and the Russian Cyrillic alphabet.

Despite the obstacles, the Concannon Rkatsiteli found a market. One day a call came in from a Russian emigré broadcaster at the Voice of America in Washington, D.C., excited that he had finally found a wine that reminded him of his home country. And the Russian Tea Room in Manhattan—famous for being "just slightly to the left of Carnegie Hall"—ordered as much as they could get from Concannon's distributor.

This offbeat wine also played a bit part in the drama of the Cold War. With tensions between the US and the Soviet Union high, atomic physicist Dr. Edward Teller hosted a group of visiting Russian scientists at the nearby Lawrence Livermore Laboratories. The lab had a "no alcohol" policy, so for a little relaxation, Teller and his guests drove over to Concannon for some bread and cheese and a little wine. Much to their surprise, the Russians were served an American Rkatsiteli, and were utterly floored. At least for one evening, the Cold War thawed a little.

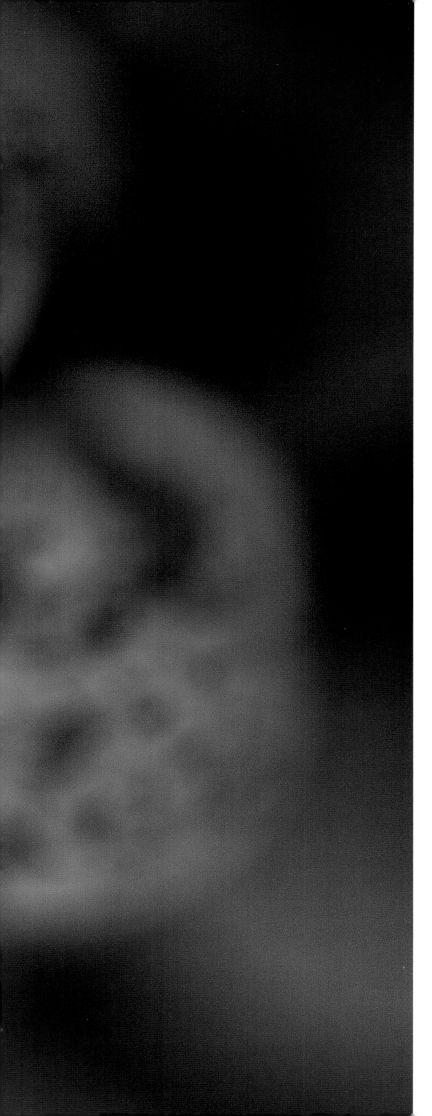

AMERICA'S FIRST PETITE SIRAH

Shortly after I became the winemaker in 1960, one of the first things my brother Joe and I did turned out to be one of the most important—and it wasn't even our idea.

Petite Sirah vines—in those days I always called it Durif—had been in our vineyards forever; some of it had been planted back in Grandfather's day. Joe paid a lot more attention to what was in the vineyard than I did. I just knew it was one of the grapes that ended up in our Burgundy blend, along with Carignane, maybe some Mourvèdre and Zinfandel, frankly I can't remember. The different blocks might be fermented separately, depending on when they came in, but they all went into the same blend. A lot of wineries made red "Burgundy" and white "Chablis" blends in those days from all kinds of grapes; they could be good wines, even though they had nothing to do with those regions in France.

One of Joe's sales contacts in southern California was a wine merchant in Pasadena named Denny Caldwell, a guy who really knew his wine, was a judge at the State Fair and so on. He would take the Greyhound bus up to Livermore and stay overnight with Joe, and they would taste and talk about wine. One night, he came up with this idea: "Why don't you keep the Petite Sirah separate and bottle it as a varietal wine, instead of putting it into the Burgundy?"

We thought it over, then waited a year, then decided to try bottling a couple hundred cases of the 1961 vintage, especially since Denny had agreed to take all of it. It was almost an afterthought for us. We didn't bother to put a vintage date on the label when we released in 1964, since vintage dating wasn't as big a deal in those days as it is now. Well, it became a hit, flew off his shelves, sold out completely. It was the first varietally labeled Petite Sirah, and it was a winner. After that, I always called Denny "Mr. Petite Sirah."

We realized that we could make a really good, distinctive wine with this grape and this vineyard. Little by little, we expanded the production, and, of course, started selling it through our other outlets and at the winery. Joe had to start scouting around California looking for more grapes to supplement what we had planted, and found some sources in Sonoma. He started knocking out other varieties and replanting our vineyards. More and more of the Petite was taken out of the old blend and bottled separately. Eventually, we just stopped doing the Burgundy altogether. But we never tried for a really big production on the Petite. We were determined to keep the quality up from one year to the next.

It became our flagship wine, the one we were known for, even though it wasn't our biggest seller. After a few vintages, we discovered that the wine could age well and develop in the bottle, and so did some of our customers who followed the wine and put it in their cellars. We caught the attention of some wine writers, locally and in other cities, who were intrigued with this almost unknown variety and impressed with what we were doing with it, especially when they realized it got better with age—which made it a more "serious" wine.

The winemaking at the beginning wasn't much different from our other red wines—crush it, use a yeast that would get it dry, ferment it for five or six days on the skins in redwood tanks, pump the wine over the skins by hand periodically, press it, and age it in large barrels—casks really—for three years. After a while, we started making a reserve Petite—we called it "limited bottling"—and put some of it in magnums and numbered the bottles. We knew if we were going to charge more, we had to focus on the best lots and make a finer wine. Today there's a lot more technology and control involved in the winemaking, of course; then we were just trying to show off the fruitiness and freshness of the grapes.

Personally, I think Petite Sirah is a better, more interesting grape than Syrah. It always has a lot of fruit to it, a lot of body. It's easy to work with as long as you don't have harvest rains, and it always ripened well here in Livermore, since it rarely rains before November. Our vines were what we called "head-pruned" in those days, looking more like bushes than the vines on trellises you see today, and that kept the tonnage of grapes down, so we had good concentration of flavors. We still farm a couple of acres of old-vine Petite that way down on Tesla Road. And it always had aging potential.

Petite Sirah used to have a reputation for being a mean wine, too tannic, especially when it was young, but we were able to make a wine that came out smooth and balanced. I'm sure aging it three years in wood before we bottled it helped get rid of the rough edges. But we also discovered that the vines planted in rocky, gravelly soil did better, the wine softened up quicker. People then—people now—didn't want something that would take the enamel off their teeth.

The main thing we did was stick with it, keep plugging, year after year. There weren't many other people who were into making Petite Sirah in those days—Foppiano in Sonoma,

Mirassou, Lee Stuart at Souverain—but we all knew we were onto something. Now there are dozens of them on the market, and ours is more sought-after than ever.

Sometimes I think Petite Sirah has a little magic to it. A couple years ago, a number of wineries that produce Petite got together for the Blue Tooth Tour, going around the country promoting the wine. Helen and I traveled in a 40-foot motor home, just for fun. When we were in Manhattan, the venue for the tasting was a small hotel, and when we got ready to leave the next morning, there was the motor home parked right in front. Turned out our driver had slipped the meter maid a bottle of Petite Sirah and got a permit sticker to hold the place overnight. In Santa Fe, where the local authorities are very particular about parking codes, there was a Lutheran Church across the street from the tasting, and we talked the pastor into letting us park there—with the help of a case of Petite.

AMERICA'S FIRST PETITE SIRAH

Petite Sirah: Finally in the Spotlight

Petite Sirah grapes have a long, distinguished history in California wine-making—almost all of it under the radar. For more than a century, it was the secret ingredient in hearty red blends, but only a handful of wineries found a way to make it shine on its own.

Petite was born in southern France in the 1880s, when nurseryman François Durif released a vine that was a cross between Syrah, the noblest red of the Rhone Valley, and Peloursin, another local variety. The new Durif grape had little success in France, but imported vines flourished in sunny California from the late 19th century on. Somewhere along the line, growers started calling it "Petite Sirah" (with several spelling variations), a name also sometimes used for Syrah itself. Over time, the grape's history and identity lapsed into controversy—was it the same as Durif? was it really just a clone of Syrah? had it originated in California? DNA testing at UC Davis in the late 1990s finally sorted out the mystery, demonstrating that almost all of California's Petite Sirah was genetically identical to Durif.

Whatever it was called, Durif/Petite's generous color and tannin made it a mainstay of mass-market field blends for decades, fermented alongside Zinfandel, Carignane, Grenache, Syrah, Alicante and whatever else might be in the vineyard. In the 1940s, Louis Martini and Larkmead briefly tried bottling it as Durif, but it didn't catch on. It wasn't until the 1960s that a few determined producers, starting with Concannon, found ways to smooth out the tannin, bring out the fruit, and showcase Petite Sirah's charms as a single-variety wine. Along with Concannon, Foppiano, Parducci, David Bruce, Fetzer, Dehlinger and Stags' Leap were among the early champions of the grape.

Only in the last few years—encouraged by the general popularity of Rhone-style wines—has Petite Sirah finally come into its own, getting the attention it deserves from dozens of labels, all up and down the price scale. It has been accepted as an official Rhone variety by the Rhone Rangers, an association of Rhone-style producers, and even has its own advocacy group, PS I Love You.

Forty years later, the wine world has caught up with Concannon.

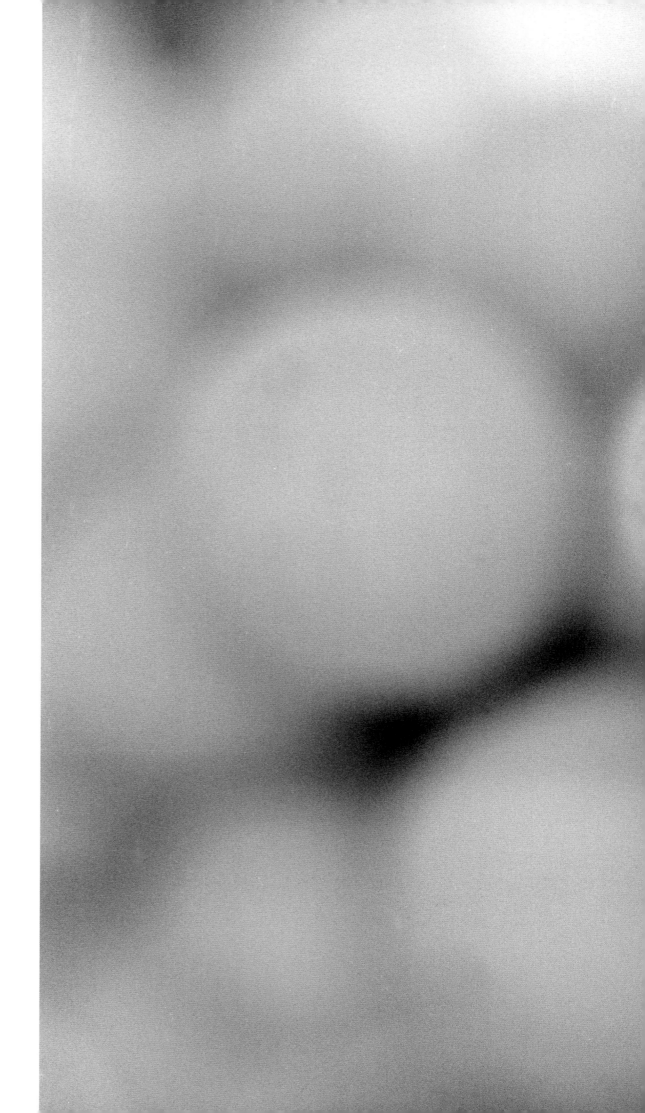

A Century Of Changing Wine Styles

Concannon Vineyard has been producing wine from the same Livermore Valley location since 1886, but the wines themselves have changed dramatically. Many of the grape varieties and wine styles which make up that bottled record have disappeared from the market and may seem old-fashioned now, but, in their heyday, these wines were as cutting edge as today's "killer" Cabernets and trendy Pinot Noirs. The history and evolution of wine styles at Concannon provides a cross-section of the development of the entire California wine industry.

The altar wines at the heart of Concannon's original lineup were all white and mainly sweet. This wasn't just the preference of the customers in the Catholic Church, but the fashion of the day—dry, red wines didn't achieve their current dominant position in the consumer marketplace until the 1960s. At the end of the nineteenth century and into the early twentieth, the Livermore Valley produced plenty of blended red wines, mostly for the lower-end mass market. But it was the whites from several wineries that planted the region's flag in the fine wine arena, attracting favorable press and new investment.

One of Concannon's signature wines for decades was its sweet, late harvest-style Chateau Y'Quem, named after the legendary vineyard in the Sauternes region of France where many of Concannon's original vine cuttings originated. The habit of naming California wines after French winemaking regions—Burgundy, Chablis—or even after specific wineries was widespread up into the 1950s. Not surprisingly, the French disapproved of the custom, and as the California wine industry grew more confident of itself, the practice largely faded away. Repackaging Chateau Y'Quem as Chateau Concannon did nothing to dampen its popularity.

Little by little, after World War II red wines took on more prominence at Concannon, in Livermore and in all of California. The notion that the Livermore Valley could only make quality white wine faded into history. Concannon had been producing blended red wine—and calling it Burgundy—for years. Cabernet Sauvignon plantings became an important part of the vineyard from the 1950s on. The success of the first Petite Sirah, released in 1964, was a turning point, signaling both more attention to reds and a turn toward bottling and labeling single-varietal wines, not generic blends.

In the 1980s, the production of altar wines finally became uneconomical and was discontinued, but dry Sauvignon Blanc and Semillon, the white grapes that had launched the winery a century before, received renewed attention. The range of wines produced was scaled back to provide more focus on mainstream varieties—Chardonnay, Sauvignon Blanc, Merlot, Cabernet Sauvignon. Petite Sirah remained a featured varietal, even as other producers were pulling vines out, because Concannon had developed such a loyal following for the wine.

In the 1990s, under Tom Lane, Concannon evolved into two wineries under one roof: the main production of standard varieties, and smaller experimental lots of Rhône varieties—Syrah, Grenache Noir, Mourvèdre, Counoise, Viognier, Marsanne, Roussanne—and Rhône-style blends. Concannon and Lane won several Winery/Winemaker of the Year awards for this combination of quality and innovation.

Concannon now has access to vineyard sources all along the Central Coast that enable it to select certain varieties—notably Pinot Noir and Chardonnay—from areas where they grow best. At the same time, the grapes that shine in this rocky stretch of Livermore soil—starting with Petite Sirah— are getting high priority, both in vineyard renovation and cellar practices. The first releases of the Heritage Petite Sirah, made from selected lots of old-vine Petite on the original Concannon property, highlight the continued emphasis on the distinctive potential of the Livermore Valley and signal Concannon's entry into the luxury wine market.

WINEMAKER TOM CONCANNON
1925-1945

WINEMAKER KATHERINE VAJDA
1950-1960

WINEMAKER JIM CONCANNON
1960-1975

WINEMAKER SERGIO TRAVERSO
1981-1989

WINEMAKER TOM LANE
1992-2003

CHANGING HANDS

In the 1970s, we were on a roll. We were growing, and we had established a national reputation for the Petite Sirah. We brought in Bob Broman, with a degree from Davis and a lot more technical knowledge, and we upgraded the fermentation and tank areas, finally catching up with the stainless steel era.

Then my brother Joe died in 1978, far too young and far too early. He was only 50, right in his prime, and it was a big, unexpected loss—to the winery, to the industry, and of course to the entire family. We had been very close, and it was devastating to me.

Joe's death meant the family had to face some difficult choices. Although only the two of us had been working at the winery, there were four siblings with equal interests—including our sisters Nina and Marie. So in 1980, the family decided to sell the winery. After nearly a hundred years of Concannons running the vineyard and living on the land, it was a painful decision, but the right thing to do was clear.

Augustin Huneeus and a group of Chilean investors, under the name Pacific Land and Viticulture, bought the vineyards and winery in 1980. They brought in Sergio Traverso as the new winemaker. Sergio was originally from Chile, too, and was the winemaker at Sterling in Napa before he came here. Giving control to someone of that caliber obviously meant a decision to keep the quality up. I stayed on, taking more responsibility for public relations and sales.

Sergio had his own definite set of ideas about winemaking. He brought in what I'd call a European angle, including more use of small barrels than we had been doing. He was a big supporter of Sauvignon Blanc and Semillon for our area and our vineyard. He came up with the name Assemblage and the concept of a proprietary blend of those two grapes, something we still make. Later on, he went over to Murrieta's Well, working with Phil Wente, and put the whole focus on those Bordeaux blends, white and red, and made some excellent wines. This was the period when many of our most visible, modern facilities got created. We turned space that had always been barrel storage into the current tasting room. Sergio had the idea of building the arbor that runs along the south side of the front lawn; it's a great place for dinners, tastings and other special events. And he's responsible for the second gate out front, the one visitors drive through when they come to the winery.

The 1980s were also a time when Concannon wine got some political visibility, national and international. Our wines were served at the White House. And when President Reagan visited Ireland in 1984, his official gift to Irish Prime Minister Garrett Fitzgerald was a Methuselah of 1979 Concannon Petite Sirah, delivered with this message: "From the young Irishman that left his homeland. He is now returning his gift."

In the decade or so Sergio was here, along with assistant winemaker Greg Upton, the winery passed through a lot of corporate hands. In 1984 Huneeus sold the place to Distillers Company Ltd., which mainly owned a portfolio of Scotch brands and made Gordon's Gin in the US. A couple years later, Distillers was taken over by Guinness—and not a very friendly takeover—which eventually merged into Diageo. Then they sold the winery off to the big German firm Deinhardt, and then Deinhardt decided to get entirely out of the US wine business, which put us up for sale again.

I think we were fortunate that all these corporate maneuvers took place so far away from Livermore. It meant we mostly got left alone. Maybe it was more of the luck of the Irish, but, through all those changes, none of the owners decided to bust up the winery and sell it in pieces or turn it into a jug-wine factory. Concannon kept its reputation for premium, quality wine, focused on Livermore, aiming to get the best possible wine from this vineyard.

When Deinhardt put the winery on the market in 1992, the new generation at Wente—Eric, Phil and Carolyn—stepped in and formed a partnership with other individuals and bought the winery. They already knew the property—it's right across the street from theirs—and of course knew the family and the traditions. They saved the winery, preserved a bit of wine history—the birthplace of Petite Sirah in America—and strengthened the Livermore Valley as a winegrowing area.

After Sergio moved over to Murrieta's Well, we had another woman winemaker—Meri Kieren. Then Tom Lane was hired. He had been at Navarro and was a terrific small-batch winemaker. Lane put more emphasis through the nineties on Rhône varieties—Syrah and blends for the reds, and Viognier, Marsanne and Roussanne for whites. A lot of these were limited production wines, mainly for our wine club members, and they were a way to carve out a Rhône niche that went along with the Petite Sirah. The main production was still Cabernet, Chardonnay, Sauvignon Blanc and Petite. Tom also introduced the red Assemblage to the lineup.

Tom brought a certain flair and sense of humor to what he did. We used to have wine club members suggest names for new releases as they came out, and somebody suggested "Call Me a Cab." So Tom came up with a label that had a yellow taxi on it and a little sign saying, "I love Concannon." Not long ago, I was doing a sales appearance in Virginia, and a woman who had been in the wine club came into the store—she still had a bottle of that wine.

In 2002, the Wentes sold the winery to The Wine Group. They're a private management-owned company with a lot of resources and the right vision for Concannon. Resources alone aren't enough. We all know the stories about important, historic wineries whose names no longer mean very much. But most of their key people live in the area, they're here for the long haul, and their plan is quality all the way. The Concannon brand should keep going for the next 125 years.

From the time we sold the winery, 25 years ago, I never left. I deal mostly with the public and with the trade, a Concannon family member who can still vouch for the Concannon brand. With our broad distribution, we frequently get calls or visits from people with the name Concannon—from the US, the UK, or our beloved Ireland. Even if there's no relationship we know of, we make them feel like family.

For half my life, I've worked for other people, but that's not how it feels. I believe in each bottle of wine. If I didn't, I wouldn't be here. I have my heart in this business. I spend my days and weekends in stores and at tastings all over the country, signing bottles and talking to people about the wine and Concannon's history—and enjoying every minute of it.

ROCKS

Grandfather would often tell his sons, "If you have nothing else to do, go pick up some rocks." We're still picking up rocks today.

The rocks in this vineyard aren't just decorative, though they do give the place a special look. They're everywhere, and they're not just on the surface. They go down 600 feet in some places, and they can be a terrific pain in the neck. But they make the vineyard what it is, they make the vines work hard, and they make the wines naturally have a lot of character.

During World War II, Dad let a company come in here and quarry gravel for the war effort, taking it from some land down by the creek that wasn't planted. When they were done, my mom insisted that they put the land back to the way it looked beforehand. Afterwards, I was never sure that this area was worth planting. But later on, these acres were bulldozed, straightened up, and developed into vineyards for Rhône varieties—it turned out there was another 30 feet of that rocky, gravely soil still there.

People always talk about the unique gates in Livermore, and Concannon has three of them, with plans to build a fourth. The "old gate"—it's about 75 years old—with the brick construction, the elaborate metal work and the "Concannon Vineyard" name in script is the most formal. It announces the place with pride, like a French château. A hundred yards farther on, the newer gate that visitors drive through is more rough and tumble like the wall that runs along the vineyards. It was built in the 1980s, and it's made out of big rocks pulled from the vineyard and cemented together. I think that gate really lets you know what this place is about. That's where you drive in, past some of the heritage Petite vines, and you can't miss the rocks by the side of the road and all around the vines. The third gate, right on the corner where the city of Livermore begins, is also made of vineyard stones. You can see vines in the foreground through this gate, and the rolling foothills of the Diablo mountain range in the background. This view has been depicted on Concannon labels for years, and it still is today.

The soil, full of these rocks, defines the wines of Concannon Vineyard. A lot of good winemakers have come and gone and the technology has changed. But this vineyard has grown excellent grapes for more than a century. Petite Sirah, sure, but Cabernet and Rhône reds, too, and first-rate whites from Grandfather's day on.

It's only going to get better. With the new replanting, better trellising, better irrigation and a new barrel room, this place is going to go into high gear. The new wines coming out are terrific. I'm on the road a lot, pouring the wines for people and opening up some new markets. The reception is great. This winery is the only place I've ever worked, and when I pull into the driveway every day it still doesn't feel like work.

Joe Heitz, a longtime friend of the family up in Napa, died about five years ago. At his memorial they gave everyone who attended a redwood seedling to take home as a memento. I don't know how many people planted them, but I made sure that tiny sapling got put in a prominent spot out in front of the winery and was taken care of. It's probably 15 feet tall now. Because of all the construction activity around here, our groundskeeper had to rescue it a while back and move it over onto the lawn by the old family house—and it's not a little tree anymore. It's just sentimental, but it's something that continues living. It's a small tie between Concannon and one of the great people and great wineries in this industry.

When I go, I don't know, maybe they'll hand out Petite Sirah vines. Or maybe just some of these rocks.

AFTERWORD: THE NEXT 125 YEARS

When The Wine Group purchased Concannon Vineyard in 2002, we knew we were acquiring an important piece of California wine history. All of us at The Wine Group enthusiastically embrace our mission to be good stewards of the beautiful Concannon estate and its vital legacy.

The histories of Concannon Vineyard and the Livermore Valley Wine Country have been intrinsically linked for almost 125 years. Both have seen eras of greater or lesser prominence on the California wine scene, but throughout the decades they have remained a constant source of first-rate grapes and distinctive wines. It is only fitting that both the winery and its region are undergoing their second quality renaissance together. That's why every bottle of Concannon wine proudly bears the words, "Established 1883 in the Livermore Valley."

As of this writing, we have passed the mid-point of a five-year project —which we call "The Next 125 Years"—to renew James Concannon's vision of a world-class estate winery. The first phase was to elevate the quality potential of the 200+ vineyard acres while ensuring that blocks of old, time-tested vines were preserved, and the best of the vine clones that Concannon pioneered were perpetuated. And yes, Petite Sirah is in the vanguard of our planning.

ARCHITECTURAL RENDERING OF BARREL AND BOTTLING ROOM COMPLEX
2006

WINEMAKER
ADAM RICHARDSON

On St. Patrick's Day 2006, the 159th Anniversary of his grandfather's birth, Jim Concannon broke ground for a new 50,000 square foot barrel and bottling room complex just west of the original winery. Captured on film by American and Irish television crews, this state-of-the-art facility should be fully operational by the 125th anniversary of the vineyard James Concannon founded.

Still to come will be the transformation of the old barrel room into a pre-prohibition wine museum, and re-dedication of the old Victorian house on the corner of South Livermore Avenue and Tesla Road in honor of James' wife, Ellen Concannon. And winemaker Adam Richardson promises to release some of our most exciting wines ever.

Although the ship has changed ownership a half dozen times since 1883, we have always been blessed to have a Concannon at the helm. We hope this continues through the fourth and fifth generations, and beyond. Come visit us and taste the proud tradition of Concannon wines.

– David B. Kent
CEO, The Wine Group

JAMES CONCANNON
2006

© Creative Camera Photography

THE CONCANNON FAMILY, THIRD, FOURTH AND FIFTH GENERATIONS
2006

CONCANNON: THE FIRST ONE HUNDRED AND TWENTY-FIVE YEARS

1883	1883-1911	1889-1904	1911	1915	1920-1933	1934	1950
JAMES CONCANNON ESTABLISHES CONCANNON VINEYARD	GRAPEVINES IMPORTED FROM BORDEAUX AND BURGUNDY	MILLIONS OF VINE CUTTINGS SHIPPED TO MEXICO	PETITE SIRAH PLANTED AT CONCANNON VINEYARD	JOSEPH S. "CAPTAIN JOE" CONCANNON TAKES OVER OPERATIONS	CONCANNON STAYS OPEN DURING PROHIBITION PRODUCING	WITH REPEAL, CONCANNON INTRODUCES CHATEAU Y'QUEM SAUTERNES-	KATHERINE VAJDA HIRED, FIRST TRAINED WOMAN WINEMAKER

1954	1960	1961	1970s-1980s	1985	1992	2002
JOE CONCANNON, JR. ASSUMES RESPONSIBILITY FOR VINEYARDS AND SALES	JIM CONCANNON BECOMES WINEMAKER	FIRST U.S. BOTTLING AND VARIETAL LABELING OF PETITE SIRAH	CONCANNON CABERNET SAUVIGNON CLONES 7 AND 8 PLANTED THROUGHOUT	WINEMAKER SERGIO TRAVERSO INTRODUCES ASSEMBLAGE® WHITE	WINEMAKER TOM LANE ADDS EMPHASIS ON RHÔNE VARIETIES	THE WINE GROUP PURCHASES CONCANNON, LAUNCHES NEXT 125 YEARS

An Old Irish Toast

May the road rise up to meet you,
May the wind be ever at your back
May the sun shine warm upon your face
And the rain fall softly on your fields
And until we meet again,
May God hold you in the hollow of his hand.